Laughing All the Way to the Blockchain: A Short Guide to Cryptocurrency & Meme Coins for Beginners

By: Tai East

Copyright Page:

Copyright © 2024 by Tai East & A SPIRIT-Kissed Soul by Tai East
https://aspiritkissedsoul.com/

All Rights Reserved. No part of this publication may be reproduced, distributed, or transmitted in any form or by any means, including photocopying, recording, or other electronic or mechanical methods, without the prior written permission of the Author/publisher, except in the case of brief quotations embodied in critical reviews and certain other noncommercial uses permitted by copyright law. For permission requests, please contact the Author on the contact page via the website listed above or via the QR code below.

Table of Contents

Chapter 1: What Is Cryptocurrency?   1

Chapter 2: How to Get Started with Cryptocurrency   8

Chapter 3: How to Choose the Right Meme Coins   14

Chapter 4: Riding the Meme Coin Roller Coaster   20

Chapter 5: Growing from Meme Coins to a Well-Rounded Crypto Portfolio   26

Chapter 6: Mastering Your Emotions in the Crypto Market   33

Chapter 7: Protecting Your Investments and Avoiding Scams   40

Chapter 8: The Future of Meme Coins and Crypto   47

Conclusion: Start Small, Learn Big --- Your Crypto Adventure Awaits   53

Glossary of Cryptocurrency Terms   58

Chapter 1: What Is Cryptocurrency?

Imagine a new kind of money that doesn't need banks, coins, or even paper. You don't carry it in your wallet—it lives entirely online. This is cryptocurrency: a fast, secure, and global way to send and receive money using the internet.

It's a bit like sending a digital letter to someone anywhere in the world, but instead of words, you're sending money. And the best part? You don't need a "middle man", like a bank, to make it happen.

Why Is It Called Cryptocurrency?

The word cryptocurrency might sound fancy, but it's really simple:

- **Crypto** means hidden or secure because it uses special technology to keep transactions safe.
- **Currency** is just another word for money.

So, cryptocurrency is secure, digital money.

How Is It Different from Regular Money?

Unlike the money in your wallet, cryptocurrency isn't printed by the government or kept in a bank. Instead, it's powered by a global network of computers that work together. Think of it as a shared system where everyone helps keep track of the money, rather than relying on one company or organization.

Another big difference? You can use cryptocurrency anywhere in the world. There's no need to exchange it for another type of money like you would if you were traveling to another country.

What Are Meme Coins?

Now let's dive into the lighter and more fun side of cryptocurrency: meme coins. You've probably come across funny memes online—those viral images or jokes that spread like wildfire and bring a smile to your face. Meme coins are cryptocurrencies born from these memes. They often begin as playful jokes or trends but have gained massive popularity thanks to the passionate and engaging communities that rally behind them.

For example, Dogecoin began as a tongue-in-cheek venture inspired by the viral "Doge" meme—a Shiba Inu dog surrounded by funny, colorful captions in Comic Sans font. In December 2013, software engineers Billy Markus and Jackson Palmer created Dogecoin as a lighthearted response to the rapidly growing world of cryptocurrencies like Bitcoin.

What started as a joke quickly became something much bigger. Dogecoin gained a loyal community and was often used for fun activities like tipping online creators or supporting charity projects. Over time, it evolved from a humorous idea into a well-known cryptocurrency with a strong fan base and a significant role in the market.

Meme coins like Dogecoin aren't just about the laughs—they've shown the power of online communities and how they can come together to create real-world impact. Their popularity often stems from a mix of humor, relatability, and accessibility, making them appealing to both newcomers and seasoned investors. While they may not always have the serious purpose of coins like Bitcoin or Ethereum, their lighthearted nature and strong communities have turned them into unexpected players in the cryptocurrency space. Meme coins remind us that crypto can be as much about fun and connection as it is about technology and finance.

Why Is Everyone Talking About Cryptocurrency?

Cryptocurrency has become a big deal because it's changing how people think about money. Here's why:

1. **It's Fast:** You can send cryptocurrency to anyone, anywhere in the world, in just seconds.

2. **It's Secure:** Transactions are protected by a technology called blockchain, which keeps everything safe and transparent.

3. **It's Accessible:** You don't need a bank account or a lot of money to get started—just a phone or a computer.

The Technology Behind It: Blockchain (Made Simple)

At the heart of cryptocurrency is something called blockchain. It might sound technical, but think of it like this...

Imagine writing down every transaction on a list that everyone can see and agree on. Once something is added to the list, it can't be changed or erased. This keeps everything honest and secure.

Instead of one person keeping the list, millions of computers around the world work together to update it. That's the blockchain—a shared system that keeps track of who owns what.

The Rise of Meme Coins

While serious cryptocurrencies like Bitcoin were created to solve problems with traditional money, meme coins are more about fun and community. They're proof that sometimes, people invest in things not just because of their value but because they enjoy being part of something bigger.

But meme coins can also be risky because their value can rise and fall quickly. We'll talk more about how to stay safe as a beginner in later chapters.

Key Takeaways

1. Cryptocurrency is digital money that's secure, fast, and works anywhere in the world.
2. Meme coins are a fun type of cryptocurrency inspired by internet trends and jokes.
3. The blockchain is a shared digital list that keeps all transactions honest and secure.

By understanding these basics, you're already taking your first steps into the world of cryptocurrency. Don't worry if it still feels a little confusing—each chapter will build on what you've just learned, making it easier to understand as we go.

In the next chapter, we'll look at how to get started with your first cryptocurrency, including choosing a wallet and making your first trade. Let's keep it simple and fun!

Chapter 2: How to Get Started with Cryptocurrency

Now that you know what cryptocurrency is, let's take the next step: how to get started.

If you've ever opened a bank account or downloaded an app, you're already familiar with the basics of what we're going to do here. The goal is to help you set up everything you need to buy, store, and manage your cryptocurrency—step by step.

Step 1: Choosing Your Wallet

Think of a cryptocurrency wallet as your digital piggy bank. It's where your cryptocurrency lives, safe and secure. There are two main types of wallets:

1. **Hot Wallets:** These are apps or online accounts that you can access on your phone or computer. They're convenient because they're always connected to the internet, but that also makes them more vulnerable to hackers. Examples of hot

wallets include MetaMask, Trust Wallet, and Coinbase Wallet.

2. **Cold Wallets:** These are offline wallets. Think of them like a USB drive for your cryptocurrency. Since they're not connected to the internet, they're much safer from cyber threats. Examples of cold wallets include Ledger and Trezor.

For beginners, starting with a hot wallet is the easiest. As you become more experienced, you can upgrade to a cold wallet for extra security.

Step 2: Picking a Cryptocurrency Exchange

A cryptocurrency exchange is like a marketplace where you can buy, sell, and trade cryptocurrencies. Some of the most beginner-friendly exchanges include:

- Coinbase
- Binance
- Kraken

When choosing an exchange, look for one that:

- Is trusted and well-reviewed.

- Offers the ability to trade meme coins if that's your focus.
- Has clear fees for buying and selling.

After you sign up, you'll need to verify your identity. This is a standard process called KYC (Know Your Customer) to ensure everything is secure.

Step 3: Buying Your First Cryptocurrency

Once your wallet is set up and your exchange account is ready, you're just a few clicks away from buying your first cryptocurrency.

Here's how it works:

1. **Deposit Money:** Link your bank account, debit card, or other payment method to the exchange. Start with a small amount to get comfortable.

2. **Choose a Cryptocurrency:** Popular options for beginners include Bitcoin, Ethereum, or a meme coin like Dogecoin.

3. **Make Your Purchase:** Enter the amount you want to buy and confirm the transaction.

Congratulations! You now own cryptocurrency. It will show up in your exchange account, but you can transfer it to your wallet for safekeeping.

Step 4: Transferring to Your Wallet

If you're using a wallet separate from the exchange, transferring your cryptocurrency is simple:

1. Open your wallet app and find your **wallet address** (it's a long string of letters and numbers, like an email address for crypto).
2. Go to your exchange account, select your cryptocurrency, and click **withdraw.**
3. Paste your wallet address and confirm the transfer.

This step ensures your cryptocurrency is fully under your control and not sitting on the exchange.

Step 5: Start Exploring

Now that you've got cryptocurrency in your wallet, you're officially part of the crypto world! Here are a few things you can do next:

- **Hold It:** Many people buy cryptocurrency as an investment, holding onto it in hopes that its value will grow over time.

- **Trade It:** If you're feeling adventurous, you can trade one cryptocurrency for another to learn how the market works.

- **Use It:** Some stores and websites accept cryptocurrency as payment. You can even send some to a friend or family member!

Tips for Beginners

1. **Start Small:** Only invest what you can afford to lose. Crypto markets can be unpredictable, and it's better to learn with small amounts.

2. **PLEASE DO YOUR RESEARCH:** Before buying any cryptocurrency, look into what it is, what it does, and why people value it.

3. **Stay Safe:** Never share your wallet password or private key. Always double-check addresses before sending cryptocurrency.

Key Takeaways

- Choose a secure wallet to store your cryptocurrency.
- Use a trusted exchange to buy and trade crypto.
- Start with small amounts and learn as you go.

In the next chapter, we'll explore how to pick the right meme coins, avoid scams, and make smart decisions as a beginner. Get ready to have some fun while staying safe!

Chapter 3: How to Choose the Right Meme Coins

Meme coins are fun, exciting, and can sometimes lead to big gains. But they can also be risky, so it's important to know how to choose the right ones. Think of this chapter as a guide to spotting the gems in the meme coin world while avoiding scams and bad investments.

What Makes a Meme Coin Worth Buying?

Unlike cryptocurrencies like Bitcoin or Ethereum, which are designed to solve real-world problems, meme coins are often created for fun or as a joke. That doesn't mean they're worthless—some have built strong communities and gained massive value. Here's what to look for:

1. **Community Support:** Meme coins owe much of their success to their communities. A strong, positive, active, and supportive community can be the driving force behind a coin's growth and popularity. To gauge a coin's potential,

explore social media platforms like Twitter, Reddit, and Telegram to assess how engaged and enthusiastic its supporters are.

2. **Real Use Cases:** While many meme coins are just for fun, some have developed practical uses, like being accepted as payment or powering a platform. A meme coin with a purpose is often more valuable.

3. **Transparency:** The team behind the coin should be open about who they are and what their goals are. Avoid coins with anonymous creators or vague promises.

4. **Popularity and Media Buzz:** Meme coins often gain value when they go viral. Look for coins that are getting a lot of attention but haven't already peaked in price.

How to Research a Meme Coin

Before buying a meme coin, it's important to do your homework. Here's a simple checklist:

1. **Visit the Official Website:** A good coin will have a professional, easy-to-understand website that explains what the coin is and how it works.

2. **Read the Whitepaper:** The whitepaper is like a business plan for the coin. It should clearly explain the coin's purpose, how it works, and its future plans.

3. **Check the Community:** Join forums or groups where people discuss the coin. Are people excited and positive, or are there complaints and warnings?

4. **Look at the Market Data:** Use websites like CoinMarketCap or CoinGecko to check the coin's price history, trading volume, and market cap. Be cautious of coins with extremely low trading volumes or sudden, unexplained price spikes.

Red Flags to Avoid

The crypto world can be full of scams, especially when it comes to meme coins. Here's what to watch out for:

1. **Rug Pulls:** This happens when the creators of a coin suddenly take all the money and disappear, leaving investors with worthless tokens. Avoid coins that seem too good to be true.

2. **Pump and Dumps:** These scams involve artificially inflating a coin's price (the pump) and then selling off their holdings (the dump), causing the price to crash. Be wary of coins with sudden, massive price jumps.

3. **No Real Information:** If a coin has no website, no whitepaper, and no clear team behind it, stay far away.

4. **Hype Without Substance:** Some coins rely solely on marketing and memes without offering anything real. Make sure the coin has a purpose or strong community support.

Diversify Your Investments

When investing in meme coins, it's smart to diversify. This means spreading your money across a few different coins instead of putting everything into one. That way, if one doesn't perform well, others might balance out your losses.

Start With These Popular Meme Coins

Here are a few meme coins that have been popular and relatively safer for beginners:

1. **Dogecoin (DOGE):** The original meme coin with a strong community and a history of being used as payment.

2. **Shiba Inu (SHIB):** Often called the "Dogecoin killer," it's grown into a major player with its own ecosystem.

3. **Pepe (PEPE):** A newer meme coin inspired by the famous Pepe the Frog meme, gaining traction quickly.

Always remember, just because a coin is popular doesn't mean it's guaranteed to succeed. Research is key!

Key Takeaways

1. Look for meme coins with strong communities, transparency, and real use cases.
2. Avoid coins with red flags like anonymous creators or sudden price spikes.
3. Diversify your investments to reduce risk.

In the next chapter, we'll dive into how to spot trends, manage your investments, and safely navigate the roller coaster ride of meme coin investing. Let's keep building your crypto confidence!

Chapter 4: Riding the Meme Coin Roller Coaster

Investing in meme coins can feel like a thrilling roller coaster ride: one moment, your investment is climbing to incredible heights, and the next, it's plunging down. This chapter will help you understand how to spot trends, manage your investments wisely, and stay safe while enjoying the ride.

Understanding the Meme Coin Market

Meme coins are heavily influenced by trends and social media buzz. Unlike more stable cryptocurrencies, their value can rise or fall based on internet hype, celebrity endorsements, or viral memes. Here's what drives the meme coin market:

1. **Community Power:** A strong, engaged community can send a meme coin "to the moon." Watch for coins with active followers on platforms like Twitter, Reddit, and Discord.

2. **Celebrity Endorsements:** When influencers or celebrities like Elon Musk tweet about a meme coin, its price can skyrocket. Keep an eye on trending topics.

3. **News and Events:** Meme coins often gain momentum when they're listed on major exchanges or announce new features. Stay updated with crypto news sites.

How to Spot Trends Early

Getting in on a meme coin before it takes off can be exciting, but it requires paying attention to the right signals. Here's how to spot a trend early:

1. **Follow the Right People:** Stay updated by following crypto influencers, meme coin communities, and trend-watchers on social media.

2. **Monitor Trending Searches:** Use tools like Google Trends or Crypto Twitter to see what coins are gaining attention.

3. **Check for Growing Communities:** Look at Reddit threads, Telegram groups, and

Discord servers. If a new coin is attracting a lot of buzz, it might be worth a closer look.

4. **Watch for Listings:** When a new coin gets listed on popular exchanges like Coinbase or Binance, it often gains significant traction.

How to Manage Your Meme Coin Investments

Because meme coins are highly volatile, managing your investments wisely is key. Here are some strategies:

1. **Set a Budget:** Decide how much you're willing to invest and stick to it. Never use any money you can't afford to lose.

2. **Take Profits Early:** If your investment doubles or triples, consider taking out your initial investment and letting the rest ride. This way, you've protected yourself from big losses.

3. **Use Stop-Loss Orders:** Some exchanges allow you to set a stop-loss order, which

automatically sells your coin if its price drops below a certain point. This can limit your losses.

4. **Don't Chase the Hype:** If a coin's price has already skyrocketed, it might be too late to jump in. Look for opportunities before they hit their peak.

Staying Emotionally Balanced

It's easy to get caught up in the excitement—or panic—of meme coin investing. Here's how to stay level-headed:

1. **Don't Check Prices Constantly:** Watching prices every minute can lead to impulsive decisions. Set specific times to check on your investments.

2. **Have a Plan:** Decide in advance when you'll buy, hold, or sell. Stick to your plan, even when emotions run high.

3. **Celebrate Small Wins:** Even a small profit is a step in the right direction. Don't feel pressured to "win big" every time.

Safety First: Avoiding Scams

The meme coin market is full of opportunities, but it's also full of scams. Here's how to protect yourself:

1. **Verify Smart Contracts:** For newer coins, check their smart contracts using blockchain explorers like Etherscan to ensure they're legitimate.

2. **Be Wary of Airdrops:** Free coin giveaways can be legitimate, but many are scams designed to steal your information or funds.

3. **Double-Check Wallet Addresses:** Always verify the wallet address when sending or receiving crypto. One wrong character can result in permanent loss.

4. **Don't Fall for Guarantees:** No one can promise you guaranteed returns in crypto. Avoid anyone making these claims.

Key Takeaways

1. Meme coin prices are driven by trends, community buzz, and market events.

2. Manage your investments by setting budgets, taking profits, and using stop-loss orders.

3. Stay emotionally balanced and avoid making decisions based on fear or hype.

4. Always prioritize safety by being vigilant against scams.

In the next chapter, we'll dive deeper into long-term strategies for navigating the cryptocurrency market as a whole, so you can confidently grow your portfolio. The goal is to move from a meme coin beginner to a more seasoned crypto investor!

Chapter 5: Growing from Meme Coins to a Well-Rounded Crypto Portfolio

By now, you've taken your first steps into the world of cryptocurrency and explored the exciting (and sometimes wild) world of meme coins. But what if you want to take your investment journey to the next level? In this chapter, we'll explore how to move beyond meme coins, build a diverse portfolio, and develop a long-term strategy for success in the cryptocurrency market.

Why Diversify?

Diversification is a fancy word for spreading your investments across different types of assets. In crypto, this means investing in a mix of coins, not just meme coins. Here's why diversification matters:

1. **Reduces Risk:** If one coin loses value, others in your portfolio might balance out your losses.

2. **Opens New Opportunities:** Different coins have different purposes and growth potential.

3. **Builds Stability:** A well-rounded portfolio is less affected by the ups and downs of any single coin.

Types of Cryptocurrencies to Consider

1. **Blue-Chip Cryptocurrencies:** These are well-established coins with a history of stability and growth. Examples include:

    - **Bitcoin (BTC):** The original and most well-known cryptocurrency, often called "digital gold" is trusted worldwide as a decentralized way to store value and make secure online payments.

    - **Ethereum (ETH):** A leading and popular cryptocurrency and platform that lets developers create apps and tools, like games and financial services, powered by secure, automatic processes called smart contracts.

2. **Utility Tokens:** These coins serve specific purposes, like powering apps or paying transaction fees. Examples:

    - **BNB (Binance Coin):** Used for trading fee discounts on Binance.
    - **Chainlink (LINK):** Connects smart contracts with real-world data.

3. **Stablecoins:** Stablecoins are tied to the value of a real-world currency (like the U.S. dollar), making them less volatile. Examples:

    - **USDT (Tether):** The most widely used stablecoin.
    - **USDC (USD Coin):** A highly trusted and regulated stablecoin.

4. **Emerging Cryptos:** These are newer projects with high potential but higher risk. Look for coins with innovative technology and growing communities.

How to Research Non-Meme Coins

The same principles you learned for meme coins apply here but with more focus on practical value.

Things to consider:

- **The Team:** Who is behind the project? Are they credible and experienced?
- **The Technology:** What problem does the coin solve, and how does it work?
- **The Roadmap:** Does the project have clear, achievable goals for the future?
- **The Community:** Even serious projects need strong community support.

Building Your Portfolio

When building your crypto portfolio, aim for a mix of coins that match your goals and risk tolerance. Here's an example of a beginner-friendly portfolio:

- **50% in Blue-Chip Cryptos (BTC, ETH):** These provide stability and long-term growth.

- **20% in Meme Coins:** Keep the fun and excitement alive while limiting risk.
- **20% in Utility Tokens:** These offer the potential for growth based on real-world use cases.
- **10% in Stablecoins:** These provide a safety net during market dips.

Strategies for Long-Term Success

1. **Dollar-Cost Averaging (DCA):** Instead of investing a large amount all at once, buy small amounts regularly (e.g., weekly or monthly). This helps reduce the impact of market volatility.

2. **Rebalancing:** Over time, your portfolio might drift from its original allocation. Rebalance by selling some coins that have grown a lot and reinvesting in others to maintain your desired mix.

3. **Hold for the Long Term:** The crypto market can be unpredictable in the short term, but many coins grow over the years.

Be patient and avoid panic-selling during market dips.

4. **Stay Educated:** The crypto world is always evolving. Follow trusted news sources, watch for updates on your favorite projects, and keep learning.

Staying Safe as Your Portfolio Grows

The more you invest, the more important it is to protect your assets:

- **Use a Hardware Wallet:** For larger investments, store your coins offline in a cold wallet like Ledger or Trezor.

- **Enable Two-Factor Authentication (2FA):** Add an extra layer of security to your exchange accounts.

- **Avoid Suspicious Links:** Scammers often target crypto investors. Only use official websites and apps.

Key Takeaways

1. Diversify your portfolio to reduce risk and increase opportunities.

2. Include a mix of blue-chip cryptos, utility tokens, meme coins, and stablecoins.

3. Use long-term strategies like dollar-cost averaging and rebalancing to grow your investments.

4. Protect your assets with hardware wallets and secure accounts.

In the next chapter, we'll explore how to navigate the emotional side of investing—staying calm during market swings, making smart decisions, and building confidence as a crypto investor.

Chapter 6: Mastering Your Emotions in the Crypto Market

Investing in cryptocurrency, especially meme coins, can be an emotional experience. The prices can soar to incredible highs or crash without warning. It's exciting, but it can also be nerve-wracking. In this chapter, we'll focus on managing your emotions so you can make smart decisions, avoid impulsive mistakes, and build confidence as an investor.

Why Emotions Play a Big Role in Crypto

The crypto market is unlike anything else. It's fast, unpredictable, and influenced by everything from global news to a single tweet. As a result, emotions like fear and greed can take over. Here's how these emotions might affect you:

1. **Fear of Missing Out (FOMO):** When you see a coin skyrocketing, it's tempting to jump in without thinking. But buying at the peak often leads to losses.

2. **Fear of Losing Everything:** Fear, uncertainty, and doubt (FUD) can cause you to panic and sell your investments during a temporary market dip.

3. **Greed:** When your investment is doing well, you might hold on too long, hoping for even bigger gains, only to watch the price drop suddenly.

4. **Excitement:** The thrill of big gains can make you take unnecessary risks, like investing more than you can afford to lose.

How to Stay Calm and Focused

The key to successful investing is learning to control your emotions. Here are some key strategies:

1. **Set Clear Goals:** Decide why you're investing. Are you saving for a specific goal, or are you experimenting with small amounts to learn? Having a purpose keeps you grounded.

2. **Create a Plan:** Write down your investment strategy, including when you'll buy, hold, or sell. Stick to your plan, even when emotions are high.

3. **Limit Your Exposure:** Only invest money you can afford to lose. Knowing that your basic needs are covered helps you stay calm during market swings.

4. **Take Breaks:** It's easy to get obsessed with watching the market, but constant monitoring can lead to stress. Check prices at set times instead of all day.

5. **Celebrate Small Wins:** Don't wait for huge profits to feel good about your progress. Celebrate every step, even if it's just learning something new.

Handling Market Highs and Lows

When the market is rising:

- Stay realistic. Prices don't go up forever, so it's smart to take some profits along the way.

- Avoid getting greedy. If you've reached your goal, consider selling a portion of your holdings.

When the market is falling:

- Don't panic. Temporary dips are normal in crypto. Selling during a dip will lock in your losses.

- Focus on the big picture. Look at your investments over weeks or months, not just days.

Practical Tools to Help You Stay on Track

1. **Price Alerts:** Use apps to set alerts for specific price changes. This keeps you informed without constantly checking prices.

2. **Budget Tracking:** Track your crypto investments separately from your regular finances to ensure you're staying within your limits.

3. **Journaling:** Write down your investment decisions and how you feel about them. Over time, this can help you recognize

emotional patterns and improve your strategy.

Learning From Mistakes

Every investor makes mistakes—it's part of the learning process. The key is to turn those mistakes into lessons.

- Did you buy during a FOMO moment? Next time, take a step back and research first.
- Did you panic-sell during a dip? Remind yourself to trust your plan and focus on long-term goals.
- Did you invest too much in one coin? Diversify your portfolio to reduce risk.

Building Confidence as an Investor

The more you learn and practice, the more confident you'll feel. Here's how to grow your confidence:

1. **Educate Yourself:** Keep reading, watching videos, and joining discussions

about cryptocurrency. Knowledge is your best tool.

2. **Start Small:** By investing small amounts, you can gain experience without the pressure of risking too much.

3. **Connect With a Community:** Joining crypto groups or forums can help you learn from others and feel less alone in your journey.

4. **Celebrate Progress:** Remember, investing is a skill that takes time to develop. Every step forward is an accomplishment.

Key Takeaways

1. Emotions like fear and greed can lead to impulsive decisions—learn to recognize and manage them.

2. Stick to a clear plan and set realistic goals for your investments.

3. Take breaks from watching the market and focus on long-term trends.

4. Mistakes are learning opportunities—use them to refine your strategy.

In the next chapter, we'll explore how to protect your investments and avoid scams, giving you the tools to invest confidently and securely. Let's continue moving forward in your crypto journey!

Chapter 7: Protecting Your Investments and Avoiding Scams

As exciting as the world of cryptocurrency is, it comes with its fair share of risks. Scammers are always looking for ways to take advantage of new and experienced investors alike. In this chapter, we'll explore how to protect your investments, recognize red flags, and safeguard your crypto journey.

Why Security Matters in Crypto

Unlike traditional banks, cryptocurrency doesn't have customer service to call if something goes wrong. Once a transaction is made, it's nearly impossible to reverse. That's why security is your responsibility.

The good news is that with the right tools and habits, you can keep your investments safe.

Essential Security Practices

1. **Use a Secure Wallet:**

    - **Hot Wallets:** Great for convenience but more vulnerable to hackers. Use only for smaller amounts of cryptocurrency.

    - **Cold Wallets:** Best for larger amounts. Since they're offline, they're virtually immune to hacking.

2. **Enable Two-Factor Authentication (2FA):** Add an extra layer of protection to your accounts. This requires you to verify your identity with a second method, like a code sent to your phone.

3. **Create Strong Passwords:** Use unique passwords for each account. Consider using a password manager to generate and store complex passwords securely.

4. **Back-Up Your Wallet:** Write down your recovery phrases (seed phrases) and store them in a safe, offline location. Never save them digitally or share them with anyone.

5. **Keep Software Updated:** Make sure your wallets and devices have the latest security updates. Hackers often exploit outdated software.

Recognizing Common Scams

The crypto world has its share of scams. Here's how to spot and avoid them:

1. **Phishing Attacks:**

    - Fake emails, messages, or websites designed to steal your information.
    - Always double-check URLs and never click on links from unknown sources.

2. **Rug Pulls:**

    - A scam where developers hype a coin, and then suddenly abandon it, leaving investors with worthless tokens.
    - Avoid coins without a clear team, roadmap, or community.

3. **Fake Giveaways:**

- Scammers promise free crypto if you send them a small amount first. This is always a trap.
- Legitimate giveaways don't require you to send money.

4. **Impersonators:**
   - Scammers pretend to be influencers or trusted figures, offering fake investment opportunities.
   - Verify accounts and never trust random offers, even if they seem to come from someone famous.

5. **Malicious Wallets or Apps:**
   - Fake apps can steal your funds once you transfer them.
   - Only download wallets and apps from official websites or app stores.

Staying Safe While Trading

When buying, selling, or trading cryptocurrency:

1. **Verify Wallet Addresses:** Always double-check the recipient's wallet address. A single typo can send your funds to the wrong place, and they won't come back.

2. **Avoid Public Wi-Fi:** Trading or accessing your wallet on unsecured networks can expose you to hackers. Use a secure, private connection.

3. **Limit Information Sharing:** Don't brag about your crypto holdings on social media or forums. It can make you a target for scams.

How to Recover from Mistakes

If something goes wrong, don't panic. Here's what you can do:

1. **Act Quickly:** If you suspect your account has been compromised, move your funds to a secure wallet immediately.

2. **Report Scams:** Share your experience with the crypto community and report scams to exchanges or platforms. This helps warn others.

3. **Learn From It:** Mistakes happen. Use the experience to improve your security habits.

Long-Term Security Tips

1. **Diversify Your Storage:** Avoid putting all your cryptocurrency in one place. Use a combination of wallets and exchanges to reduce risk and protect your assets.

2. **Use Trusted Exchanges:** Stick to well-known platforms with strong security measures.

3. **Stay Educated:** The crypto world evolves quickly. Keep learning about new scams and security practices to stay ahead.

Key Takeaways

1. Security is your responsibility—use strong passwords, secure wallets, and enable two-factor authentication.

2. Watch out for scams like phishing attacks, rug pulls, and fake giveaways.

3. Always verify wallet addresses and avoid trading on public Wi-Fi.
4. Learn from mistakes and stay updated on the latest security practices.

Now that you know how to protect your investments and avoid scams, it's time to look ahead. What's next for the world of cryptocurrency and meme coins?

In the next chapter, we'll explore the exciting possibilities that lie ahead, from innovations in blockchain technology to the growing role of meme coins in the digital economy. The crypto world is constantly evolving, and understanding its potential will help you stay ahead of the curve. Let's dive into the future!

Chapter 8: The Future of Meme Coins and Crypto

The cryptocurrency landscape is one of constant change, innovation, and surprise. Meme coins, born from humor and internet culture, have become a unique part of this world, blending financial speculation with community-driven creativity. As we look to the future, one question stands out: where do meme coins and cryptocurrency go from here?

In this chapter, we'll focus on what the future might hold, highlighting emerging trends, potential shifts, and the exciting possibilities that lie ahead.

Meme Coins: What's Next?

Meme coins have already defied expectations by evolving from jokes to digital assets with massive followings. Here's where they might be heading:

1. **More Utility:** As the crypto market matures, meme coins may develop practical uses. Imagine being able to use

your favorite meme coin to access online platforms, tip creators, or even make charitable donations. Utility could turn these playful coins into tools for real-world impact.

2. **Deeper Integration into Web3:** The rise of Web3—the next generation of the internet—offers meme coins a chance to play a larger role. Meme coins could become integral to decentralized platforms, gaming economies, and digital marketplaces.

3. **Evolving Communities:** Communities are the heartbeat of meme coins, and their influence will likely grow. These groups may gain more control through decentralized governance, shaping how meme coins are used, developed, and distributed.

4. **Creative Ecosystems:** Beyond currency, meme coins could power creative ecosystems, funding digital art, NFTs, and innovative projects. They could serve as the financial backbone for a new and

revolutionary wave of creativity and internet culture.

The Bigger Picture: Cryptocurrency's Future

Cryptocurrency as a whole is poised to impact industries far beyond finance. Here's what might shape the future:

1. **Mass Adoption:** From individuals to global corporations, more people and organizations are embracing crypto. Payment processors, retailers, and even governments are exploring ways to integrate blockchain technology into daily life.

2. **Blockchain Advancements:** Newer, faster, and more energy-efficient blockchains are being developed, which could make cryptocurrency more sustainable and accessible. These advancements will open doors to applications we can't even imagine yet.

3. **Decentralized Everything:** Decentralization is a core principle of crypto, and it's spreading. From social

media to finance, decentralized systems are challenging traditional institutions, empowering users to take control.

4. **Regulation's Role:** Governments worldwide are grappling with how to regulate cryptocurrency. Clearer rules could bring stability and legitimacy, but they might also challenge the decentralized ethos that crypto was built on.

How You Can Prepare for the Future

The evolving nature of crypto means staying adaptable is key. Here's how to position yourself for what's to come:

1. **Stay Informed:** Follow credible crypto news sources, join online communities, and keep up with developments in blockchain technology.

2. **Look for Emerging Trends:** Keep an eye on how meme coins are being used and how new cryptocurrencies are entering the market. Being early to a trend can offer exciting opportunities.

3. **Focus on Your Goals:** The crypto space will always be dynamic, but having clear personal goals—whether it's learning, investing, or connecting—will keep you grounded.

4. **Think Long-Term:** While meme coins are fun, balance them with investments in projects with strong fundamentals. A mix of playfulness and stability will set you up for long-term success.

Key Takeaways

1. Meme coins could evolve into tools for creativity, utility, and community-led innovation.

2. The broader cryptocurrency landscape is moving toward mass adoption, decentralization, and blockchain advancements.

3. Staying informed, curious, and adaptable will help you navigate the ever-changing crypto world.

The future of meme coins and cryptocurrency is unwritten, full of possibilities limited only by our imagination. Whether you're in it for the fun, the potential profits, or the thrill of being part of something revolutionary, you're already a part of shaping this exciting movement.

Conclusion: Start Small, Learn Big — Your Crypto Adventure Awaits

Congratulations on concluding this journey! What an incredible adventure it's been—exploring the basics of cryptocurrency and diving into the playful yet dynamic world of meme coins. You've gained the knowledge to confidently step into this exciting new frontier.

This isn't just the end of a guide—it's the start of your journey. The crypto world is expansive, brimming with opportunities, challenges, and limitless potential. By taking small steps, staying curious, and embracing the process, you can confidently step into this ever-evolving landscape.

Reflecting on Your Crypto Journey

Take a moment to appreciate how far you've come. You've learned:

1. **The Basics:** Cryptocurrency is digital money powered by blockchain technology, offering speed, security, and global access.

2. **The Role of Meme Coins:** These fun, community-driven coins have proven their worth through viral trends, creative communities, and surprising value.

3. **Smart Investing Strategies:** From setting up wallets and choosing exchanges to diversifying your portfolio, you've mastered the essentials of responsible investing.

4. **Emotional Resilience:** Understanding how to manage fear, greed, and hype ensures you make thoughtful decisions, even in volatile markets.

5. **Staying Safe:** With strong security habits and an awareness of scams, you're prepared to protect your investments.

Every concept and tip you've learned is a building block for your success.

The Power of Starting Small

The world of cryptocurrency can feel overwhelming, but starting small is your secret weapon. By experimenting with small investments, you can:

- Learn the ropes without unnecessary risk.
- Gain confidence as you see how the market works.
- Make mistakes that teach valuable lessons without major consequences.

Remember, even the most experienced investors started where you are today—taking small steps toward a bigger vision.

Keep Learning, Keep Growing

Cryptocurrency is ALWAYS evolving, and there's always more to discover. Whether it's exploring new coins, keeping up with blockchain innovations, or understanding emerging trends, the learning never stops.

- **Stay Curious:** Follow trusted news sources, join online communities, and ask questions.

- **Stay Flexible:** Be open to new opportunities and ready to adapt to changes.

- **Stay Patient:** Crypto is a marathon, not a sprint. Long-term success comes from steady, thoughtful investing.

Your Adventure Awaits

Now it's your turn. With everything you've learned, you're ready to take action. Start by:

- Setting up a wallet if you haven't already.
- Exploring meme coins and other cryptocurrencies.
- Connecting with communities to share ideas and gain insights.

Crypto isn't just about money—it's about innovation, creativity, and being a part of something bigger. By joining this movement, you're helping shape the future of finance and digital culture.

A Final Word of Encouragement

The cryptocurrency journey might seem overwhelming, but you've already taken the most important step: deciding to learn. Every question you ask, every coin you research, and every decision you make brings you closer to becoming a confident and successful investor.

Your future in cryptocurrency shines as brightly as the path you choose to create— and your journey is just beginning. So, start small, dream big, and enjoy every step of the way! Who knows— with curiosity, research, persistence, and the right strategy, you might just find yourself laughing all the way to the bank! Or in the world of crypto, shall we say laughing all the way to the blockchain?! LOL! Happy investing!

Glossary of Cryptocurrency Terms

Here's a simple glossary of key terms to help you navigate the world of cryptocurrency. Keep this handy as a quick reference!

Airdrop: A marketing strategy where free cryptocurrency is distributed to users, often as part of a promotion or to build a community.

Altcoin: Any cryptocurrency other than Bitcoin. Examples include Ethereum, Dogecoin, and Shiba Inu.

Blockchain: A decentralized digital ledger that records all cryptocurrency transactions across a network of computers. Think of it as a public list that ensures transparency and security.

Cold Wallet: A type of cryptocurrency wallet that is not connected to the internet, making it highly secure. Examples include hardware wallets like Ledger and Trezor.

Cryptocurrency (Crypto): Digital money that uses blockchain technology for secure and decentralized transactions.

Decentralized: A system that isn't controlled by a single authority, like a government or bank, but instead by a network of users.

Exchange: A platform where you can buy, sell, and trade cryptocurrencies. Popular examples include Coinbase, Binance, and Kraken.

FOMO (Fear of Missing Out): A common feeling in crypto where investors rush to buy a coin because they fear missing out on potential profits.

FUD (Fear, Uncertainty, and Doubt): Negative information or rumors about a cryptocurrency that can cause panic and lead to price drops.

Gas Fees: Transaction fees paid to process transactions on a blockchain. They're especially common on the Ethereum network.

HODL: A slang term in the crypto community meaning "Hold On for Dear Life." It refers to keeping a cryptocurrency investment for the long term despite market volatility.

Hot Wallet: A cryptocurrency wallet connected to the internet, like apps or online accounts. Convenient but more vulnerable to hacks.

Market Cap: The total value of a cryptocurrency, calculated by multiplying its price by the number of coins in circulation.

Meme Coin: A cryptocurrency inspired by internet memes or jokes, often driven by community hype rather than practical uses (e.g., Dogecoin, Shiba Inu).

Mining: The process of verifying cryptocurrency transactions and adding them to the blockchain. Miners are rewarded with new coins.

Private Key: A secret code that allows you to access and control your cryptocurrency. Never share it with anyone.

Public Key: A code that acts as your "crypto address" for receiving funds. It's safe to share with others.

Pump and Dump: A scam where the price of a coin is artificially inflated ("pumped") so scammers can sell at a high price, causing the value to crash ("dump").

Rug Pull: A scam where developers hype a coin, then abandon the project and run off with investors' money.

Smart Contract: Self-executing contracts with terms directly written into code. These are commonly used on the Ethereum blockchain.

Stablecoin: A type of cryptocurrency that is tied to the value of a real-world currency, like the U.S. dollar, to reduce price volatility (e.g., USDT, USDC).

Token: A type of cryptocurrency that represents an asset or utility, often built on an existing blockchain like Ethereum.

Wallet: A digital tool that stores your cryptocurrency. It can be a hot wallet (online) or a cold wallet (offline).

Whitepaper: A document that explains the purpose, technology, and goals of a cryptocurrency project.

www.ingramcontent.com/pod-product-compliance
Lightning Source LLC
Chambersburg PA
CBHW071429220526
45469CB00004B/1460